On with the Shrew!

A One-Act Farce
Adapted From
William Shakespeare's
TAMING OF THE SHREW

By

BILL VAN HORN

THE DRAMATIC PUBLISHING COMPANY

****

*** NOTICE ***

The amateur and stock acting rights to this work are controlled exclusively by THE DRAMATIC PUBLISHING COMPANY without whose permission in writing no performance of it may be given. Royalty fees are given in our current catalogue and are subject to change without notice. Royalty must be paid every time a play is performed whether or not it is presented for profit and whether or not admission is charged. A play is performed anytime it is acted before an audience. All inquiries concerning amateur and stock rights should be addressed to:

DRAMATIC PUBLISHING
P. O. Box 129, Woodstock, Illinois 60098.

(ON WITH THE SHREW!)

ISBN 0-87129-515-6

ON WITH THE SHREW!

A One-Act Play

for Five Men, Six Women, Extras

CHARACTERS

MIKE (Gremio). . . . . .a student actor

MRS. SHUBERT . . . . .the high school Drama Director

BERNIE (Baptista) . . . . .a student actor

MORGAN (Woman Four) . . . . .a student actress

JUDY (Woman Two) .a student actress

RON (Petruchio). . . . . .president of the Drama Club

TERRI ANN (Kate). . . . . Ron's girlfriend, an actress

VALERIE (Woman One) . . . . .a student actress

BIANCA . . . . .sweet sister of Kate

LUCENTIO and HORTENSIO. . . . . Bianca's suitors

MAIDENS, PAGES, MUSICIANS,
MERCHANT, MONK, CUPID . . . . Extras

Time: The Present and The Past
Place: A high school stage

ON WITH THE SHREW !

SCENE: A high school stage that holds scenery representing the medieval town of Padua.

AT RISE OF CURTAIN: Some of the ACTORS dressed in period costumes and other ACTORS in regular clothes scurry across the stage. They ad lib such phrases as "Hurry up!" "What time is it?" and "Is your mom coming?" MIKE, in costume, is alone on the set fixing some scenery as MRS. SHUBERT dashes across the stage carrying a clipboard.

MRS. SHUBERT (glancing at her watch). Hurry, Mike! Only five minutes until curtain time. (She waves off L.) Harriet! Harriet! I've found your stocking! (She dashes off L.)

(TERRI ANN enters R in costume.)

MIKE. Hi, Terri Ann.

(MORGAN, in regular clothes, and JUDY, in costume, peer out from behind the scenery.)

TERRI. I'm not speaking to you! (She turns away.)
MIKE (perplexed). Why not? That note you put in my locker said that you wanted to go to the prom with me.

TERRI. I didn't write that note and I didn't put it in your locker!

MIKE (putting his hands on Terri's shoulders). Now wait a minute!

(RON enters L in costume.)

RON. Well, pardon me! (To MIKE.) I ought to punch in your face!

MIKE (backing off). Oh, don't do that.

RON. Why?

MIKE. You'll spoil my makeup. (He hurries off R.)

RON. Boy, Terri, you're something else!

TERRI. Listen to me, Ron –

RON (interrupting). No.

TERRI. I didn't write that note to Mike.

RON. It had your name on it, didn't it?

TERRI. I'm telling you, I didn't write it! I've never lied to you.

RON. There's always a first time. I'll never believe you again!

TERRI. Please, Ron . . . (She goes to RON.)

RON (pushing TERRI away). Just get out of my way.

TERRI. That suits me just fine. And you get out of my life! (She stomps off L. RON exits R.)

(MORGAN and JUDY come out from their hiding place. MORGAN carries a pretty gown.)

MORGAN. Ha, ha! That will teach Terri Ann to leave my boyfriend alone.

JUDY. Your boyfriend? Don't be ridiculous, Morgan. Ron doesn't know you exist.

MORGAN. Well, he will soon enough.

JUDY. I wonder who wrote that note to Mike? It was a dirty trick.

MORGAN. I wrote it.

JUDY. You what?

MORGAN. I wrote the note to Mike and signed it with Terri's name.

JUDY (shocked). But why? What has Terri ever done to you?

MORGAN. Are you kidding, Judy? First she gets the leading role in the play – and then she gets to kiss Ron at the end of the play. That's rotten.

JUDY. Terri didn't write the play. Shakespeare did.

MORGAN. Well, he's rotten, too. Anyway, she'll be sorry. (She takes a can from the gown and sprinkles powder from it on the gown.)

JUDY. What are you doing?

MORGAN. Sprinkling itching powder on this gown.

JUDY. Morgan, stop it! That's Terri's gown!

MORGAN. Right. I was supposed to wear it, but old sourpuss Shubert gave it to Terri. Ha, ha, I'll show Terri! (She puts more powder on the gown.)

JUDY (looking off L). Watch it. Here comes Mrs. Shubert. (MORGAN hides the can and the gown behind her back.)

(MRS. SHUBERT enters L.)

MRS. SHUBERT. Oh, Morgan. I've got good news for you.

MORGAN. Terri Ann can't be in the play?

MRS. SHUBERT. No. But I want you to wear the gown she was supposed to wear. You know, the gown you fussed so much about.

MORGAN. Why do I have to wear it?

MRS. SHUBERT. Because I found another one for her.

MORGAN. But I don't want to wear it anymore.

MRS. SHUBERT (angrily). No buts! You complained all week about not being able to wear it. Now put it on and hurry up! Do you hear me?

MORGAN. Yes, Mrs. Shubert. (She starts off R. JUDY laughs.)

MRS. SHUBERT. Why are you laughing, Judy?

JUDY. Oh, never mind. (She exits with MORGAN who is trying to shake the powder out of the gown. MRS. SHUBERT buries her nose in the clipboard.)

(BERNIE enters L, barefooted and in costume.)

BERNIE (nervously). Er . . . Mrs. Shubert?

MRS. SHUBERT. What's wrong now, Bernie?

BERNIE. I can't find my horse.

MRS. SHUBERT. How in heaven's name could you lose a horse? Perhaps I should have given you an elephant. Go and find it! (BERNIE slumps off R.)

(TERRI enters L, crying.)

MRS. SHUBERT. What's wrong, Terri Ann?

TERRI (sobbing). I'm not going to be in the play.

MRS. SHUBERT. Now, now. Don't be nervous.

TERRI. I'm not nervous. I hate Ron!

MRS. SHUBERT. But I thought you were good friends.

TERRI (sobbing). I hate him!

MRS. SHUBERT. But you and Ron have the leading parts in the play! It isn't just any actress who gets to play the part of Kate in *The Taming of the Shrew*. You're a good actress, Terri Ann, and we're all counting on you. (To the audience.) Oh, be still my bleeding ulcer.

TERRI (drying her tears). All right – but I won't kiss him! I'll never kiss him again, ever!

MRS. SHUBERT (as TERRI runs off sobbing). But that kiss is the high point of the play!

(BERNIE enters R.)

BERNIE. Guess what, Mrs. Shubert.
MRS. SHUBERT. What, Bernie?
BERNIE. I found my horse.
MRS. SHUBERT. Well, heigh-ho, Silver!
BERNIE. But . . .
MRS. SHUBERT. Don't say but, Bernie. I hate it when you say but.
BERNIE. I can't find my shoes. I think somebody hid them.
MRS. SHUBERT. Well, find them! (BERNIE rushes out R.)

(RON stomps in R. MRS. SHUBERT fans herself with the clipboard.)

RON. I'm not going to be in the play.
MRS. SHUBERT. And I say that you are! (She points DC.) Out there – out there on the other side of the closed curtain are about five hundred people – good people who have paid good money to see a good performance. And . . . (She shakes her finger at RON.) . . . buster, it was your idea to present this souped-up, jazzed-up, cool version of Shakespeare, not mine! So, do it!
RON. All right. But I won't kiss her at the end of the play!
MRS. SHUBERT. But Petruchio always kisses Kate.
RON. This Petruchio isn't! (He exits L.)
MRS. SHUBERT. This cast doesn't need me, it needs Ann Landers. (She looks at her watch.) Good grief! (She calls off.) Places! Places, everyone!

(GREMIO, LUCENTIO, HORTENSIO, WOMAN ONE, and RON enter. RON stands C. LUCENTIO, GREMIO, and HORTENSIO sprawl at L. WOMAN ONE carries a broom and stands a little to the right of and behind RON. ALL are nervous.)

MRS. SHUBERT. Good luck, everybody. Break a leg! (She gazes heavenward, then runs off L.)

WOMAN ONE. I'm so scared, I think I'm going to die.

HORTENSIO. Why? You've only got five lines.

WOMAN ONE. I know. And I've forgotten every one of them.

RON. Quiet. The curtain is going up. (ALL freeze. After a few seconds, RON clears his throat, steps forward, and bows. To the audience.) Welcome, everyone, to the Drama Club's version of Shakespeare's *Taming of the Shrew*. We've changed it here and there, and there and here we've stuck with the original. And, now, we proudly present *On With The Shrew*! (He gestures and runs off R. The lights come up full as the "performance" begins. WOMAN ONE sweeps vigorously over to GREMIO, LUCENTIO, and HORTENSIO.)

WOMAN ONE. Wake up! Wake up! Here in Padua, it's morning.

HORTENSIO (sitting up). Here in Padua, it's boring. (GREMIO snores.)

LUCENTIO (sitting up). Hear, hear. Gremio is snoring.

HORTENSIO (collapsing). Another boring . . .

LUCENTIO (collapsing). Morning.

(WOMAN TWO runs in R.)

WOMAN TWO. A stranger rides into town!

WOMAN ONE. Bring all the maidens down. A good man is hard to find.

WOMAN TWO. And harder yet to keep, I've found. (She runs off L. WOMAN ONE peers off R.)

(WOMAN TWO reappears R with WOMAN THREE and the MAIDENS.)

WOMAN THREE. What news is there, I pray you tell, that sweeps o'er town like some clear bell?

WOMAN ONE. A stranger comes on yonder steed. Why, it is he. Yes, he indeed. Baptista comes with all his wealth.

GREMIO (springing up). Wealth?

WOMAN TWO. Aye, wealth. Everything he touches, I am told, turns to silver or to gold.

LUCENTIO (springing up). Gold!

WOMAN THREE. Aye, gold. Why, he makes more money than bees do honey.

WOMAN ONE. He has two daughters, I am told.

HORTENSIO (springing up). Daughters!

WOMAN ONE. Aye, daughters. One is sweet, the other sour. One is happy, the other dour.

HORTENSIO. Names, woman!

LUCENTIO. Give us names!

GREMIO. So we can play our wooing games!

WOMAN TWO (as the MEN listen intently). Bianca is the nicer of the two. Kate, the older, is Kate, the shrew.

WOMAN THREE. See, now they come!

(ALL are excited as BAPTISTA, barefooted, rides in R on his "horse." He throws coins to ALL and rides over to L.)

WOMAN ONE. Baptista there doth look the blues.

BAPTISTA. And well he should – he's lost his shoes.

(KATE in her sedan chair is carried in R by two male PAGES.)

HORTENSIO (leaping over to KATE). Bianca! (He bows.) Welcome to our town. (KATE snorts and hits him on the head. He falls.)

WOMAN ONE. She is not Bianca. See her frown.

LUCENTIO (crossing to KATE). You must be Kate. You've knocked him down. (He bows.)

KATE. Out of my way, you grinning clown! (She knocks LUCENTIO down.)

GREMIO (approaching KATE). Art thou really Kate, the shrew?

KATE. My name is Katherine. Out of my way!

GREMIO (on bended knee). Nay, stay.

KATE. Away, I say – away! (She knocks GREMIO down, then claps her hands and the PAGES carry her chair over to BAPTISTA.)

(BIANCA in her sedan chair is carried in R by two male PAGES.)

BIANCA. I beg thee, pardon her, my sister. She hates all those whose name is mister. But men to me are not so frightful. (She smiles.) Indeed, I find you most delightful.

HORTENSIO (springing up). Delightful Hortensio! (He bows.)

LUCENTIO (springing up). Delightful Lucentio! (He bows.)

GREMIO (springing up). And more than delighted Gremio! (He bows too low and falls over.)

BAPTISTA (calling to BIANCA). Come, Bianca, we must away. You'll see them yet another day.

BIANCA (holding out her hand so the MEN can kiss it). Parting is such sweet sorrow. Adieu, adieu, adieu. See you tomorrow. (She waves to the MEN as the PAGES carry her L.)

MEN (on their knees, waving). Until tomorrow. Until tomorrow. Until tomorrow.

KATE (mimicking the MEN). Until tomorrow. Until tomorrow.

BIANCA (as the MEN blow her kisses). See that! See that! They blow me kisses!

KATE (throwing a scathing look at the MEN so that they hiss). Hear that! Hear that! They throw me hisses. (She puts her fingers in her ears and gives the MEN a Bronx cheer. ALL gasp. She and BIANCA are carried off L, followed by BAPTISTA and the MEN. The OTHERS follow.)

(After a short pause, a loud commotion is heard off L. GREMIO, HORTENSIO, and LUCENTIO run on, pursued by an angry KATE who brandishes a rolling pin. BAPTISTA and a weeping BIANCA follow them on.)

BAPTISTA. Gentlemen, gentlemen, please – please! Bianca cannot marry until I . . . (He looks heavenward.) . . . have a husband for Katherine. (He slides his foot forward in an emotional manner and picks up a splinter.) Ouch! (He holds his foot and hops around.)

LUCENTIO. Katherine must marry first?

BAPTISTA (holding up his foot). Yes. (The MEN groan. BAPTISTA groans as he tries to remove the splinter.) And if any of you love Katherine, you have my permission to court her at your pleasure. (He puts his foot down and grimaces.)

LUCENTIO. Court her? Cart her, rather. She's too rough for me. (BAPTISTA again attempts to remove the splinter from his foot.)

KATE (shaking the rolling pin at LUCENTIO). In faith, sir, you shall never need to fear. For if I cared at all, my care should be to comb your noodle with a three-legged stool and paint your face, and use you like a fool! (She turns abruptly and stalks off L, followed by a weeping BIANCA and a limping BAPTISTA.)

LUCENTIO. How shall we get that hellcat married off?

GREMIO. Better far that she be carried off!

LUCENTIO. Away – away with her!

HORTENSIO. How far away?

LUCENTIO (singing to the tune of *Dixie*). Away.

GREMIO (singing). Away.

MEN (singing). Away down south in Sicily!

GREMIO. Aha! Aha! The time is hot for us to carry out a plot! (The MEN huddle briefly, then exit R, chortling.)

(KATE enters from L with the weeping BIANCA.)

KATE. Come dry thy tears, thou weeping wench, and get thee from the mourner's bench! It grates my ears to hear thy wails for loss of thy insipid males! (There is a commotion offstage R.)

BIANCA. Hark! Someone comes.

(The three MEN enter R in masks and carrying sacks. They stalk KATE.)

GREMIO (holding up his bag). Ha! Ha! We've come to get you, Kate! Witch! Shrew! Prepare to meet thy fate!

MEN. Aha! Aha! Aha! (They attempt to bag KATE.)

KATE (eluding the MEN). Oh, help! Oh, help! Pity me a maid – alone and helpless and afraid!

LUCENTIO. You'll soon be in the bag! Never more to nag!

BIANCA. Help! Oh, help! I'm frightened through and through!

HORTENSIO (as he and the OTHERS comfort BIANCA). Fear not! Fear not! We mean no harm to you!

GREMIO. Because of Kate, we're quite irate. We're going to do her in. Take her away, so we can stay, and try your love to win. (The MEN stalk KATE again.)

(WOMAN FOUR enters from R with a broom. She scratches herself constantly. KATE runs to her.)

KATE. Lady, lady, may I stay? (She hides behind WOMAN FOUR.) I am hunted. I am prey! Save me from the hounds that bay. Let me live another day!

WOMAN FOUR. Nay, nay, go away. For your sins you have to pay. (She scratches herself with the broom.) Oooohh! (She runs off R.)

KATE (continuing to run from the MEN, then looking off R and becoming herself again). Wait, Kate! Kate, wait! I cannot believe my ears that I should utter such foolish fears.

(A MERCHANT pushes in a pushcart from R. KATE draws herself up bravely and goes to the MERCHANT. She picks out a large frying pan from the merchandise on the cart, then speaks to the MEN as the MERCHANT exits.)

KATE. What? Thinkst thou thus to knock me down and hustle me swiftly out of town? I'll strike a blow for E.R.A. . . . (She hits LUCENTIO who crumples to the floor.) . . . for me . . . (She hits GREMIO who falls down.) . . . and Helen Gurley Brown! (She hits HORTENSIO who collapses.)

LUCENTIO (holding his head). Alack, alack, my head doth crack.

HORTENSIO (holding his back). I fear that she hath broke my back.

GREMIO (feeling his jaw). Forsooth, forsooth, five teeth are loose! The little vixen's cooked our goose! (The MEN groan. KATE exits L, laughing.)

HORTENSIO. We must get a husband for Katherine.

GREMIO. A husband? A devil!

LUCENTIO. I say a husband.

GREMIO. I say a devil!

HORTENSIO. Then let's away and plan anew a way to give the devil Kate, his due. (The MEN exit L.)

(Ron, as PETRUCHIO, enters R on a "horse" and rides to C.)

PETRUCHIO. Verona, for a while I take my leave to see my best friends here in Padua but, most of all, my best-beloved and approved friend, Hortensio!

(HORTENSIO enters from L.)

HORTENSIO. How now, my good friend, Petruchio? (He and PETRUCHIO clasp hands.) What happy gale blows you to Padua from Verona?

PETRUCHIO. Such winds as scatter young men through the world to seek their fortunes further than at home. And I have thrust myself into this maze, happily to wive and thrive as best I can. Therefore, if thou knowst one rich enough to be Petruchio's wife, tell me.

HORTENSIO (gleefully). I can, Petruchio, help thee to a wife with wealth enough and young and beauteous. Her only fault – and that is fault enough – is that she is intolerably shrewish. Such a life with such a wife were strange, even though there's money in it.

PETRUCHIO. It matters not. Lead me to her – and tell me more. (He and HORTENSIO exit L.)

(KATE enters L and crosses to C. PETRUCHIO, on foot, enters and goes to KATE.)

PETRUCHIO. Good morrow, Kate. For that's your name I hear.

KATE. Well have you heard, but somewhat hard of hearing. They call me Katherine that do speak of me.

PETRUCHIO. You lie, in faith, for you are called plain Kate. And bonny Kate and, sometimes, Kate the curst. But Kate, the prettiest Kate in Christendom. And hearing thy mildness praised in every town, thy virtues spoke of and thy beauty sounded, myself am moved to woo thee for my wife.

KATE. Moved? In good time. Let him that moved you hither remove you hence! Beware my sting, Petruchio.

PETRUCHIO (bowing). Good Kate, I am a gentleman.

KATE. Then, gentleman, prepare to try my sting! (She hits PETRUCHIO.)

PETRUCHIO. I swear I'll cuff you if you strike again.

KATE. If you strike me, you are no gentleman.

PETRUCHIO. Nay. Come, Kate, you must not look so sour.

KATE. It is my fashion when I see a crab.

PETRUCHIO. Why, here's no crab and, therefore, look not sour.

KATE. There is. There is.

PETRUCHIO. Then show it me.

KATE. Had I a looking glass, I would. Out of my way! (She moves R.)

PETRUCHIO (blocking KATE). Nay, stay and hear me. 'Twas told me you were rough and coy and sullen. But I find you pleasant, gamesome, passing courteous, slow in speech, yet sweet as springtime flowers.

KATE. Where did you study all this goodly speech?

PETRUCHIO. I've made it from my mother's wit.

KATE. A witty mother! Then how came her son to be so witless?

PETRUCHIO. Enough! Your father's consented that you will be my wife and the dowry's agreed upon. Come kiss me, Kate!

KATE. Never! Never! (She kicks at PETRUCHIO but he holds her off.)

(BAPTISTA enters L, limping.)

BAPTISTA. How goes the wooing, Petruchio?

PETRUCHIO (holding off an angry KATE). Very well, sir. In fact, we have so well agreed that Sunday is our wedding day.

(A MUSICIAN carrying a lute strolls in from L.)

KATE (breaking away from PETRUCHIO and taking the lute from the MUSICIAN). I'll see you hanged on Sunday first! (She slams the lute over Petruchio's head and runs off R.)
PETRUCHIO (to BAPTISTA). Your daughter is quite musical, sir.
BAPTISTA (examining his foot). How so?
PETRUCHIO. She hath brought music to my ears. (He pulls the lute off his head and gives it back to the MUSICIAN who examines it sadly, then exits R.) Now, let's away for Sunday is my wedding day! (He and BAPTISTA exit L. There is a blackout for several seconds to denote the passing of time. As the lights come up again, PAGES carry an archway out to C. Other PAGES bring in a small table and place a punch bowl and a piece of wood on it.)

(BIANCA, GREMIO, HORTENSIO, and LUCENTIO dance in.)

BIANCA. Oh happy, happy wedding date! Today Petruchio marries Kate!

(MUSICIANS enter with instruments. They play as WOMEN ONE, TWO and THREE enter, along with other GUESTS.)

WOMAN ONE. They say Baptista's happy with his daughter.
WOMAN TWO. I've heard that she goes like a lamb to slaughter.
WOMAN ONE. They say pity him who takes Kate to wife.
WOMAN TWO. I've heard she'll make him miserable all of his life!
WOMAN THREE. They say that in Petruchio she'll meet her match no matter how she doth kick and scratch.

(CUPID leaps across the stage scattering flower petals, then exits. The GUESTS mull around and appear to be bored. KATE, in her wedding gown, arrives. She is quite obviously concerned. BAPTISTA, limping, enters with the MONK. He holds up his foot and the MONK tries to remove the splinter.)

KATE. The wedding march has sounded much. The musicians' arms are numb. (BAPTISTA yells as the MONK finally removes the splinter.) And my own father yells and rails , while I do worry and bite my nails. But the bridegroom doth not come. Oh, what has happened? Where is he? I'm waiting at the church! I fear that crafty Petruchio has left me in the lurch! (She stomps her foot angrily and paces back and forth. BAPTISTA smiles as the MONK holds up a splinter of wood about six inches long.)

MONK (crossing to the angry KATE). Peace, sister, peace. It is thy wedding day.

KATE (pushing the MONK away and going to the table). Peace? Peace? Aye, I'll give him peace! (She picks up the piece of wood.) The peace of gentle slumber! (She brandishes the piece of wood.) I'll hit him peacefully with this large piece of lumber! And with this stock, I'll make him rock! (She puts down the wood and picks up the punch bowl.) And from this punch, he'll roll! He'll say "hello" when he gets slopped with all this liquid jello!

(PETRUCHIO enters L in a ragged tunic and jaunty cap with a long feather in it.)

PETRUCHIO (chiding KATE). Kate, oh, sweet Kate? My darling Kate? Oh, wherefore hast thou tarried? Oh, I have waited oh, so long, to see thee and be married. The wedding feast is growing cold. We've got the priest a'guessing. Methinks we must begin at once or he'll withhold his blessing. (He takes Kate's arm.)

KATE (pulling away). No! By my soul, I will not marry thee! (She crosses to the other side of the stage and pouts.)

BAPTISTA (limping over to KATE and falling on his knees). Canst thou not pity me?

KATE. Pity thee? Oh, father, pity me, pity me! To marry such a rogue as this.

PETRUCHIO. 'Twill be heaven! 'Twill be bliss! (KATE snarls at PETRUCHIO and turns away.)

BIANCA (running to KATE). Oh, sister, sister, list to me! And grant to me thy sympathy. If thou weddst not, then I cannot. I will an old maid be! (She weeps. GREMIO, HORTENSIO, and LUCENTIO affect a position of grief.)

KATE (sighing). Dry thy tears, Bianca, and father, off thy knees. I'll sacrifice myself, the both of you to please. (She helps BAPTISTA off the ground.)

BAPTISTA. Ah, such a lovely daughter. (Joyfully.) Let the wedding now go! And let the music start to flow! (The MUSICIANS play an aria by Mendelssohn or some similarly appropriate piece.)

PETRUCHIO. What? Callst thou that music?

KATE. Aye. The sounds are pleasing to my ear.

PETRUCHIO. Bah. Sounds like that I do not wish to hear.

KATE. But they are soft and sweet as wedding songs should sound.

PETRUCHIO. Bah. Music like that is heard when they put you in the ground. (He walks over to the MUSICIANS.) Wake up, thou sleepy musicians! Wake up and play a tune! And make it frantic, make it hot, and make it last 'till noon! So play the jive, make us alive! We'll have a little disco like our brothers and sisters do out there in San Francisco! (The MUSICIANS play a modern number. ALL dance. The lights flicker on and off. After a few minutes, the music ends. KATE and PETRUCHIO stand together under the arch. BIANCA is the maid of honor and HORTENSIO is the best man. The MONK reads from his book.)

MONK. Dearly beloved.

PETRUCHIO. I love thee, Kate.

MONK. We are gathered together.

KATE. You are a rogue. (She kicks PETRUCHIO.)

MONK. To join together this man and this woman in holy matrimony.

PETRUCHIO. Ouch! Must kick me now? (He elbows KATE.)

MONK. It is therefore not to be entered into unadvisedly.

KATE. Ouch! I'll advise thee! (She hits PETRUCHIO on the head.)

MONK. Into this estate these two persons come to be joined.

PETRUCHIO. And I'll join thee! (He hits KATE on the head.)

MONK. No other human ties are more tender.

KATE. Ouch! Thou art heavy-handed! (She kicks PETRUCHIO.)

PETRUCHIO. And thou art heavy-footed. Oohh! (He hops around.)

MONK. Will you, Petruchio, love, honor, and protect her?

PETRUCHIO. Protect her? Zooks! Who will protect me? (He grabs KATE, pulls her to a chair, and paddles her.)

MONK (as KATE struggles free). And, Kate, will you keep him in sickness and in health?

KATE. Keep him? Ha! You can have him. I don't want him. (She pats her behind.)

MONK. Who giveth this woman to be married?

BAPTISTA. I do.

CROWD. We do!

MONK. Give her the ring.

PETRUCHIO. Ring? Aye, I will. (HORTENSIO hands him a

very large wire necklace with a bell hanging on it. PETRUCHIO places it around Kate's neck.)

KATE. What am I to do now? Moo?

MONK. And hast thou a ring for him?

KATE. I have. (She smacks PETRUCHIO on the head and bells ring offstage.)

MONK. Thou hast given him a ring!

PETRUCHIO. She has rung his chimes.

KATE. I'd rather wring his neck.

PETRUCHIO. You scrounge! (He hits KATE.)

KATE. You nit! (She kicks PETRUCHIO. He hops. KATE holds her head.)

MONK. I now pronounce you man and wife. (ALL ooh and aah.) You may kiss the bride.

PETRUCHIO. Nit! (He hits KATE in the head again.)

MONK. I said you may kiss the bride.

KATE. Scrounge! (She kicks PETRUCHIO. BOTH fall to the floor and groan. PETRUCHIO holds his leg. KATE holds her head.)

WOMAN ONE. Such a lovely couple.

WOMAN TWO. They were made for each other.

WOMAN THREE. Aye. The crippled bridegroom and the battered bride.

KATE (getting up). Tell me, tell me, how looks the carriage that we will ride this day of our marriage?

PETRUCHIO (getting up). The carriage is a thing of beauty, a joy forever. Overlaid with fairest gems, garnished with silver and gold. Fit for a princess such as yourself, thy beauteous self to hold.

KATE. I beg of thee, please let me see this carriage madest for me. That I, a bride, might ride in pride to wherever I must be.

PETRUCHIO. Behold! Your carriage waits.

(A PAGE pushes in a wheelbarrow filled with hay. A "Just Married" sign hangs on the wheelbarrow.)

KATE. What? I see only a wheelbarrow.

PETRUCHIO. And I say it is a carriage!

KATE. Where, then, are the horses?

PETRUCHIO. It is a horseless carriage.

KATE. And what shall draw such a carriage?

PETRUCHIO. We shall have to draw upon our resources, madame.

KATE. Meaning that . . . (She climbs into the wheelbarrow.) . . . you will push me!

PETRUCHIO. Meaning that . . . (He pushes KATE out of the wheelbarrow and climbs in himself.) . . . you will push me!

KATE (angrily, with her hands on her hips). You push me too far, sir!

PETRUCHIO. Nay. I have not pushed you at all. But, come now, you push me.

KATE. I'll push you, indeed. Over the brink! (She picks up the handles and dumps PETRUCHIO out of the wheelbarrow onto the floor.)

PETRUCHIO. Hey, there!

KATE. Hay is right. (She throws hay at PETRUCHIO.) Hey, nonny, nonny.

PETRUCHIO. And a hot cha-cha! (He throws hay at KATE. BOTH laugh and continue to throw hay at each other. ALL join in.)

MONK. Methinks this is the best reception I've been to in years!

KATE (on the floor next to PETRUCHIO). Oh, Petruchio! (She laughs.) What fun!

PETRUCHIO (laughing). Oh, Kate, my bonny Kate. How I love thee!

KATE. And I love thee, Petruchio.

PETRUCHIO. Thou art not angry at me?

KATE. Nay. Art thou angry at me?

PETRUCHIO. No. I love you, Terri, er, I mean Kate. (ALL laugh.)

KATE. And I love you, Ron, er, Petruchio. (She laughs.)

PETRUCHIO. Aye. There's a wench! Come kiss me, Kate!

KATE. I come, but not because thou orderest me. I come because I want to. I love thee. (She and PETRUCHIO kiss. Bells ring.)

HORTENSIO, GREMIO, LUCENTIA. At last! At last! Bianca's free! (The MEN go to BIANCA and kneel.) Marry me! Marry me! Marry me!

BIANCA (pointing to each of the MEN). Eenie, meenie, minee, mo. Which one to marry? Which ones let go? (She exits L and the MEN eagerly follow her.)

KATE. And now, Petruchio, come kiss me!

PETRUCHIO (laughing). Aye. And I come, but not because thou orderest me. I also come because I want to. I love thee. (He and KATE kiss.)

(As one kiss leads to another and another, MRS. SHUBERT storms onstage.)

MRS. SHUBERT. For heaven's sake, close the curtain! Close the curtain!

CURTAIN

PRODUCTION NOTES

COSTUMES

Present day and medieval period. Mrs. Shubert wears glasses, a dark skirt and blouse. Her hair is in a bun. Kate changes into a wedding gown. The Pages should be dressed alike if possible. The Monk wears a long robe and cowl. Cupid carries a small bow, arrows, and flower petals. The Merchant has a tattered tunic. Petruchio has a "Robin Hood" hat with feather.

PROPS

Two cardboard or wooden horses. Two sedan chairs. Brooms. A wheelbarrow or cart. A "Supermarket" sign for the Merchant's cart. Burlap bags. Masks. Gold pieces. Stools. Benches. A punch bowl. A long piece of wood. A book. An arch with a stained glass window effect to represent the church. Lutes, horns, harps for the Musicians. A clipboard. A splinter. A wheelbarrow full of straw or shredded yellow paper. A large wire necklace with a cow bell attached. Flower petals. A box of itching powder. A rolling pin. A small table. A lute. A "Just Married" sign.

LIGHTS

Slightly dim when the play starts. Up full when the play-within-the-play begins. Disco effects during dance sequence.

SOUND EFFECTS

Taped or live music where appropriate.

Simple drapes may be used to make the stage look "Shakespearean" if the medieval village scenery presents a problem.

DIRECTOR'S NOTES

DIRECTOR'S NOTES

DIRECTOR'S NOTES

DIRECTOR'S NOTES

DIRECTOR'S NOTES

DIRECTOR'S NOTES

DIRECTOR'S NOTES